NUMEX BIG JIM

HABANERO

NUMEX SUNGLO

HUNGARIAN PAPRIKA

CAYENNE

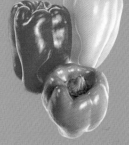

BELL PEPPER

TABASCO

ANCHO

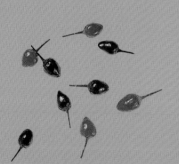

PRETTY PURPLE

NEW MEXICO

NUMEX SUNFLARE

NUMEX ECLIPSE

WITHDRAWN

YELLOW WAX

ROCOTO

NUMEX SUNBURST

CHILE FEVER
A CELEBRATION OF PEPPERS

STORY AND PHOTOGRAPHS BY ELIZABETH KING

DUTTON CHILDREN'S BOOKS ● NEW YORK

SPECIAL PHOTO CREDITS
p. 13: The pimiento and pasilla photographs © 1992
The Chile Institute.
p. 16: The Nazca bowl photograph © 1994
The Metropolitan Museum of Art.

Library of Congress Cataloging-in-Publication Data

King, Elizabeth, date
Chile fever: a celebration of peppers/story and photographs
by Elizabeth King.—1st ed.
p.   cm.
ISBN 0-525-45255-9
1. Hot peppers—New Mexico—Hatch Region—Juvenile literature.
2. Hatch Chile Festival, Hatch, N.M.—Juvenile literature.
3. Hatch (N.M.)—Social life and customs—Juvenile literature.
4. Hot peppers—Juvenile literature.
[1. Hot peppers.   2. Hatch Chile Festival, Hatch, N.M.
3. Hatch (N.M.)—Social life and customs.]   I. Title
SB307.P4K55   1995   641.3'384—dc20   94-31279   CIP   AC

Published in the United States 1995 by Dutton Children's Books,
a division of Penguin Books USA Inc.
375 Hudson Street, New York, New York 10014

Designed by Amy Berniker

Printed in Mexico
First Edition
1 3 5 7 9 10 8 6 4 2

FOR MY CHILE QUEEN AND BELOVED MOTHER,
MARTHA DAWSON KING

This book gave me the opportunity to return again to the pleasures that New Mexico routinely offers—the comforting smell of piñon wood burning in fireplaces, the taste of blue-corn enchiladas smothered in spicy red chile sauce, and the views of salmon-colored hills dotted with scrubby sagebrush—like living O'Keeffe paintings.

I would like to thank Dr. Paul "The Chileman" Bosland of New Mexico State University for his knowledge and generous spirit; Debbie Wilson, of the Hatch Chamber of Commerce; Dr. James King, Ellen Stone, and Elyssia Stratton for their photo assistance; Val and Ray Wilkinson; Martha King; Kathleen and Tom Minor; Susan Hazen-Hammond and Eduardo Fuss for their friendship and knowledge of chiles and photography; photographer Josh Margolies for his generosity and talent; and Susan Van Metre and Lucia Monfried of Dutton Children's Books for their wonderful guidance.

I would also like to thank the following people and establishments for their kindness and participation in this project: Victor Espinosa; The Chile Institute; the Flores Farms; Eliseo and Margaret Flores; Rhonda, Falicia, and Ricardo Armendariz; the Jackalope Station, the Hatch Chile Express; Elizabeth Berry, the Gallina Canyon Ranch; Jody Cooper; Gary Gutierrez; The Chili Pepper Emporium; The Christmas Shop; Bobbi Lane; Robert Dunn; Sophia, Sampson, and Derek Huang; the Bombay Gate; Sanjay, Tanvi, Roshni, Dhruv, and Rutu Vyas; Isaic and Christopher Duran; Leo Madrid; Frutas San Lorenzo; the San Miguel Mission; The Inn at Loretto; Andrea Roye; Misty Weathers; The Mesilla Valley Inn; Max Gonzalez Salán; Tom Dormody; Eloisa Mendez; and the people of Hatch, New Mexico.

Big hugs for my family—Dale, Taylor, and Claire Ettema—for understanding and for eating all those fast-food dinners.

It is the end of summer. All along the roadsides near Hatch, New Mexico, there are signs of chile fever. In the fields of this fertile valley near the Rio Grande, bright red chile peppers are ready to be harvested. Thousands of chiles will be picked for shipping, and some will be placed on the rooftops of Hatch to dry in the sun.

For a few days each year, the little New Mexican town becomes the chile pepper capital of the world. The Hatch Chile Festival is a celebration of the town's favorite crop.

In late February or early March, the farmers plant the chile seeds. They grow into neat rows of two-foot-tall bushes. By July, the pepper pods have developed. These green pods begin to ripen and turn red in August.

Some pods are harvested in midsummer while they are still green. The rest are not picked until the end of the season when the peppers are bright red and the flowers in nearby fields are in full bloom.

The chile peppers grown by the farmers of Hatch are shipped all over the country. They are used to make the salsa that is stacked in colorfully labeled jars on grocery shelves. They are heaped on plates of nachos in restaurants and baseball parks. And they are made into red powder that spices up bowls of home-cooked chili con carne, the stew of meat and beans that gets its name from chile peppers. Chiles make all of these foods taste hot to the tongue.

BELL PEPPER

JALAPEÑO

NEW MEXICO

Jalapeños, bell peppers, and New Mexico green chiles are the most common peppers in American meals, but there are actually over three thousand varieties of chile peppers that grow worldwide.

Right down the road from Hatch, Dr. Paul Bosland of New Mexico State University raises hundreds of kinds of chiles. He finds varieties that will grow well locally. By breeding one type of chile with another, he can create new varieties. Dr. Bosland develops some just for their beauty, like these NuMex Twilight chiles.

Peppers are usually thought of as vegetables, but the pods are really fruits or berries. They are part of the nightshade family, which includes eggplants and tomatoes.

Chile peppers come in many colors, sizes, and shapes. They can be red, orange, yellow, white, green, purple, brown, or black. And most chiles change color as they mature.

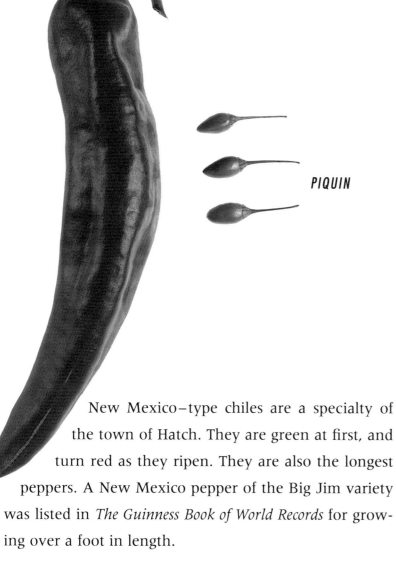

NEW MEXICO

PIQUIN

Among the smallest chiles is the piquin; several could fit in the palm of your hand. And there are also small, round peppers like the cascabel. Its name means "little rattle," for the sound the seeds make when it is dried.

CASCABEL

New Mexico–type chiles are a specialty of the town of Hatch. They are green at first, and turn red as they ripen. They are also the longest peppers. A New Mexico pepper of the Big Jim variety was listed in *The Guinness Book of World Records* for growing over a foot in length.

PASILLA

MIRASOL

The spike-shaped red mirasol pepper grows pointing upward—its name is Spanish for "looking at the sun." There are even heart-shaped peppers like the pimiento, which is used to stuff green olives.

PIMIENTO

The pasilla pepper is long and thin. It is a favorite pepper in Mexico, where it is dried and combined with chocolate and other ingredients to make a delicious brown sauce called mole.

But the truly special thing about chiles is their fiery taste. A chemical in the inner walls of the pepper pods gives them their heat. It is called capsaicin. Different kinds of chiles have different amounts of capsaicin. Chile peppers that have less capsaicin than others do not tend to taste as hot. Some chiles, like the bell pepper and the pimiento, have no capsaicin. They are not hot at all.

When capsaicin touches the tongue or skin, it causes a burning sensation. The human body reacts to the pain by releasing a painkilling chemical that also gives a slight, overall feeling of well-being. That is why so many people enjoy eating peppers despite their blistering heat.

Many Americans consider the jalapeño pepper very hot, but it is mild compared to the world's hottest chile. The habanero pepper from Mexico is sixty times hotter than the jalapeño!

HABANERO

It is only lately that chiles have become such a popular part of the American diet. Salsa, which is made from chopped peppers, tomatoes, onions, and herbs, is now used as a food topping more often than ketchup.

Recent immigrants from other countries have introduced new dishes made with peppers to America. Indian and Chinese meals are so notoriously hot that many people think chile peppers originally came from Asia. But chiles are actually native to the Americas. Scientists believe that the ancestor of chile peppers first grew millions of years ago in what is now Bolivia.

Chile peppers were a common crop in the New World when Columbus arrived in 1492. The Nazca people of Peru were growing peppers more than a thousand years ago. Chiles were so important to their diet that the Nazca painted images of them on bowls and other pottery. And peppers were not just used as food. The Aztecs paid taxes with pepper pods, using them as a sort of money.

Columbus noticed the chiles and thought he had discovered the same strong spice Marco Polo had found in the Far East called black pepper. So Columbus gave chiles the name "pepper." When the Spanish arrived in Mexico a little later, they borrowed the Aztec name for the pods, *chilli*, which means "red." They eventually changed the word to *chile*, and now the pods are known by many as chile peppers.

Europeans carried chile peppers from the New World back to the trading centers of Europe and Africa. The peppers spread around the world in just one hundred years. They were quickly adopted by many countries into their cuisines.

Today they are especially valued in countries where the main diet consists of plain, starchy foods like rice, corn, and potatoes. Peppers give these bland meals exciting heat and flavor.

Farmers in New Mexico have cultivated chiles for many years. The Flores family has grown chile peppers for several generations. This year's harvest is good. Ricardo has gathered some tasty green New Mexico chiles to show his great-grandfather Mr. Eliseo Flores. Many green chiles have been picked to be sold during the Hatch Chile Festival.

Mr. Flores checks the rows of bushes for chiles that have turned pinto, which means they are beginning to show spots of red. They will be harvested when they have changed color completely. Chile peppers can be eaten when they are green or red.

Isaic Duran and his brother Christopher have set to work early roasting a variety of green New Mexico chiles called Sandías. The brothers are getting these peppers ready to sell at their family's produce stand.

Though Christopher likes to bite into fresh, whole Sandías, most people prefer the peppers with their tough skins removed. To loosen the skin, the boys roast the chiles in a large mesh drum that they turn over a propane gas jet. Isaic spins the drum quickly so that the chiles will cook evenly. The chile skin begins to blister, and the boys know that the peppers are fully roasted.

With gloved hands, Isaic shovels the warm chiles into a plastic bag. The heat of the chiles inside the closed bag makes the pods "sweat" and loosens the skin. Now it can be peeled off. The chile peppers are ready to be eaten.

During the harvest season, New Mexico is full of chiles—and they are not all for eating. The chiles are also used for decoration. They are a symbol of a good harvest.

Every home, church, restaurant, and store is fes-
tooned with garlands of red chiles called ristras. Farmers
sell ristras at roadside stands.

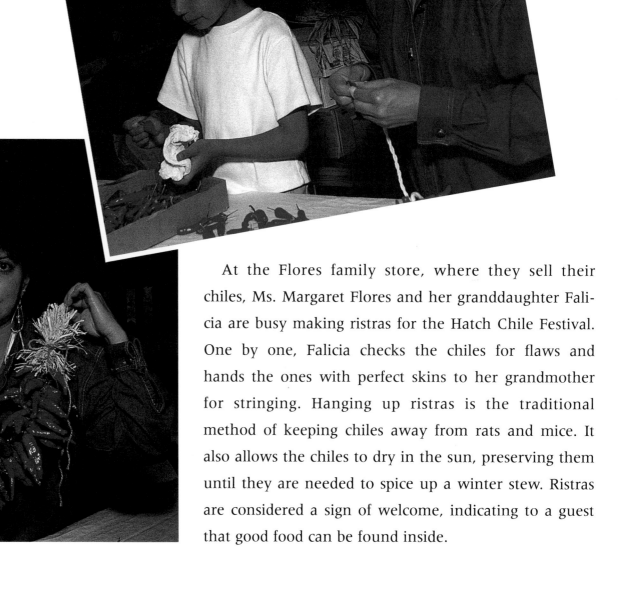

At the Flores family store, where they sell their chiles, Ms. Margaret Flores and her granddaughter Falicia are busy making ristras for the Hatch Chile Festival. One by one, Falicia checks the chiles for flaws and hands the ones with perfect skins to her grandmother for stringing. Hanging up ristras is the traditional method of keeping chiles away from rats and mice. It also allows the chiles to dry in the sun, preserving them until they are needed to spice up a winter stew. Ristras are considered a sign of welcome, indicating to a guest that good food can be found inside.

Chiles are everywhere! There are handblown chile Christmas ornaments, chile jewelry, chile lights, chile ceramics, chile piñatas, and even chile dolls to hug. And the cooks in the town of Hatch are busy making batches of salsa and chili con carne for the hungry visitors arriving for the festival.

The festival begins with a parade. Native Americans in traditional clothes, horses, men in Civil War uniforms, floats, and baton twirlers march down the main street of Hatch. The townspeople and visitors follow the parade out to the festival grounds.

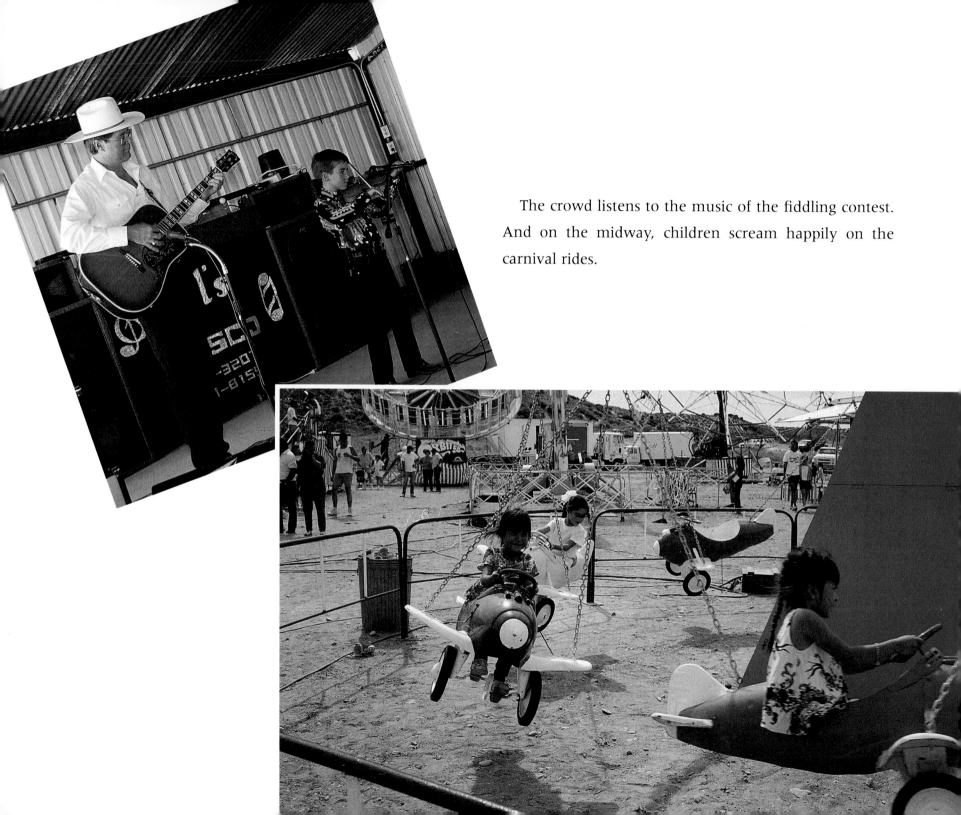

The crowd listens to the music of the fiddling contest. And on the midway, children scream happily on the carnival rides.

Between activities, people sample the many dishes that have been prepared with basketfuls of harvested New Mexico chiles. There are salsas, stews, casseroles, pizzas, and hamburgers—all made with chiles. Judges choose the best pepper recipe. It is chiles rellenos, fried green peppers stuffed with cheese.

They also crown two festival queens—the Green Chile Queen and the Red Chile Queen. The winners, wearing green and red dresses, stand before the crowd and read their essays on chile peppers.

Dr. Bosland comes to the festival to judge the most serious contest. He chooses the best-shaped pepper pod from those grown by the farmers. The seeds from the prizewinning pepper will be saved to plant in next year's crop.

The first day of the festival is almost over. Everywhere people are eating the chiles that they have worked all year to grow. And elsewhere in the world, millions of people are adding chile peppers to their food for the sheer thrill of savoring their unique heat and flavor.

¡VIVA LOS CHILES! HURRAY FOR CHILES!

CHILE PEPPER NOTES

MEASURING CHILE PEPPER HEAT

Different types of chile peppers have different levels of heat. The heat is caused by a chemical called capsaicin. Scientists can measure the amount of capsaicin in individual peppers and tell exactly how hot each one is. One method was created by a pharmacist named Wilbur L. Scoville. He took a precise amount of chile pepper and diluted it with a liquid solution. The more liquid that had to be added for the heat to be undetectable to the human tongue, the hotter the chile. Based on this method, chiles are assigned a number, called Scoville Heat Units, according to the amount of liquid required to dilute them. The bell pepper scores zero Scoville Heat Units, while the jalapeño rates from 2,500 to 5,000 Scoville Heat Units. But it is the fiery habanero that usually scores highest, with 100,000 to 300,000 Scoville Heat Units!

HOW TO SAY CHILE PEPPER NAMES AND OTHER WORDS

cascabel: *kas-kah-BELL*

habanero: *hah-bah-NEH-roh*

jalapeño: *hah-lah-PEHN-yoh*

mirasol: *mee-rah-SOHL*

pasilla: *pah-SEE-yah*

pimiento: *pee-MYEN-toh*

piquin: *pee-KEEN*

Sandía: *san-DEE-ah*

capsaicin: *kap-SAY-ah-sin*

mole: *MOH-leh*

piñata: *peen-YAH-tah*

pinto: *PEEN-toh*

rellenos: *reh-YEH-nohs*

ristra: *REE-strah*

¡Viva los chiles!:

    VEE-vah lohs CHEE-lehs

CHILE PEPPER HEAT SCORES

VARIETIES	SCOVILLE HEAT UNITS	VARIETIES	SCOVILLE HEAT UNITS
Big Jim	500–1,000	pasilla	1,000–1,500
cascabel	1,500–2,500	pimiento	0
habanero	100,000–300,000	piquin	30,000–50,000
jalapeño	2,500–5,000	Sandía	1,500–2,500
mirasol	2,500–5,000		

A CHILE PEPPER RECIPE

GREEN CHILE ROLL-UPS

You will need:

1 four-ounce can of chopped green chiles

1 eight-ounce container of soft or whipped cream cheese

1/4 teaspoon of garlic powder

4 flour tortillas

plastic wrap

Open the can of green chiles and press the lid against the chiles to squeeze out the extra water. In a large bowl, stir together the chiles, cream cheese, and garlic powder.

Using a spatula or knife, spread the mixture on the four tortillas. Roll them up tightly and wrap them in plastic wrap. Place them in the refrigerator for about three hours. Then unwrap them. The roll-ups are ready for eating. They can also be sliced into bite-size snacks by cutting across each roll several times.

NUMEX BIG JIM

HABANERO

NUMEX SUNGLO

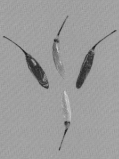

HUNGARIAN PAPRIKA

CAYENNE

BELL PEPPER

TABASCO

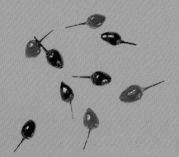

PRETTY PURPLE

ANCHO

NUMEX SUNFLARE

NEW MEXICO

NUMEX ECLIPSE

ROCOTO

NUMEX SUNBURST

YELLOW WAX